FOLLOW YOUR DREAMS AND CHANGE YOUR LIFE:
THE KEYS TO MOVING FROM A DREAMER TO A DREAM MAKER
BY: CLINTON W. MITCHELL, ESQ.

ACKNOWLEDGMENTS

First, and foremost, I'd like to thank God for the opportunity to share my work with the world. I'd also like to thank my parents, Charles and Sharon Mitchell, for being the best parents a kid could ever ask for. I'd like to thank my wife Piper for her love and patience. Last, but not least, I want to thank my family, friends and colleagues for their support. I love you all.

CWM

TABLE OF CONTENTS

INTRODUCTION

In order for us to make sense of our daily lives, we segregate, differentiate, identify and label everything and everyone; so much so that we spend more time sorting our differences than we do realizing our many similarities. For example, we all have thoughts, feelings and emotions that drive us to do whatever it is that we do. While many believe that the notion that everything happens for a reason is just a cliché to help you deal with the unexplainable, it's not; in fact, it's actually a truism. Just because we don't know or understand the reason behind why something happened doesn't make it unexplainable. It simply means that the answer has not yet been made aware to us, which leads to another one of our similarities. Attempting to make sense of the unknown is also one of the things we all have in common.

Another common trait that people share is that we all have dreams. Rich, poor, Black, White, Hispanic, genius or blockhead, we all have dreams. Some people dream of being superheroes, others dream of hitting the winning shot and many dream of simply being successful. We even dream of having the perfect mate, house, sports car, or the possibility of running the world. While what we dream about varies from person to person, the commonality is that we all dream. But what are our dreams made of?

Dreams are successions of images, ideas, emotions and sensations that occur involuntarily in the mind during sleep.[1] Austrian neurologist Sigmund Freud, responsible for developing the discipline of psychoanalysis, wrote extensively about dream theories and interpretations. Freud believed that dreams are a manifestation of our deepest desires and anxieties, often relating to repressed childhood memories or obsessions.[2] In other words, the things that we desire, covet, obsess about or repress are the ideas, emotions and sensations that will visit us in our dreams.

What visits you while you're sleeping? What do you dream about? What do you covet, desire, or obsess about? What do you want most out of this world? Is it the brand new pair of designer jeans you may eat your way out of in a week? Is it a limited edition pair of tennis shoes that will lose their value the moment you put them on your feet? Or is it that special someone you see every day but have yet to work up the nerve to speak to? Are these the images that you see in your dreams? Do these things illicit vivid emotions beyond your control? Are these the things your dreams are made of; the things you want the most?

Many of us pursue the things we dream about, but what if your dreams were bigger? What if you dreamed less about things that will give you temporary happiness and more about things that will grow with you and give you life-long joy? Things such as a good education, a fulfilling career, love, happiness, helping to end world hunger, healing the sick and touching the lives of those less fortunate than you. Imagine how different your dreams would be if those were the things that you wanted most out of life.

In Disney's *Pirates of the Caribbean*, the lead character, Captain Jack Sparrow owned a compass. Only this was no ordinary compass. Instead of pointing north, the compass would point in the direction of the thing the person holding it desired most. Imagine what you could do with a compass that would lead you to whatever you wanted most. Although there would still be the problem of getting the gold out of Ft. Knox or getting

Beyoncé or Chris Hemsworth to go on a date with you, but at least you would know in what direction to travel to try to make these things happen. How much simpler would life be if, at the very least, you knew in which direction to travel, what path to take, what turn to make, and what bridge to steer clear of to avoid the troll and get to what you desire most? The answer: much easier.

We don't need Captain Jack Sparrow's magic compass or any of Disney's movie magic to point us in the direction of the things we desire most. Our minds serve as our compass, our roadmap, and our GPS to take us wherever we want to go. If we let our dreams be our guide we can do whatever we want, within reason. Flying without the aid of an airplane, helicopter or space shuttle are examples of dreams not within reason. However, absent the absurd or ridiculous endeavors, there isn't much we can't do. But we must have a plan.

The plan is to dream it, believe it and do it. It's not enough to dream about dating the captain of the cheerleading squad if you never introduce yourself and ask for her number. It makes no difference to dream of scoring the winning touchdown if you don't believe that you can achieve it. It's pointless to come up with the world's greatest idea if you never follow through on it. A great idea must be matched with action. Anatole France said, "To accomplish great things, we must dream as well as act." If you can dream it, you can do it. You start with the dream, pair it with the belief that you can do it and then do it. Dream it. Believe it. Do it. It's just that simple.

The lessons in this book are for people of all ages, but they are especially geared towards millennials. The three main reasons I chose to focus on this group are: (1) I don't think enough people speak directly to them; (2) Youth and young adults are the world's greatest asset; and (3) My publisher told me to. When you have something you care about, you invest in it: children, a charity, a car, or a house. When you invest in it with your time, energy and money, it appreciates in value.

To me, the youth and young adults of this world are our greatest commodity, much more valuable than any gem, stone or precious metal. Since this is my firmly held belief, I am committed to investing in them and in us. I believe we should spend money on programs and groups that educate them and enrich their lives. We should take the time to show them that we care by spending time with them. We should share our talents and skills with them so that when our time on this planet draws to a close, there are people behind us who can still repair a carburetor, sing opera, build houses and recite the lyrics to "Rapper's Delight". Because of my belief in young people, their potential and their power, I wrote this book to speak directly to them, to you, about how you can cultivate, nurture and transform your dreams into reality.

I believe there are five steps to getting what you want out of life and following your dreams. I believe there are five steps that separate the dreamers from the dream makers. There are five steps that will be the difference between just dreaming about what you want and realizing what you want. In the following pages, we will explore all five steps in great detail, and I am convinced that once you read this book in its entirety, foreword, table of contents, credits and all, you will be ready to follow your dreams and go from being just a dreamer to a dream maker.

"If you can dream it, you can do it."
-Walt Disney

CHAPTER 1: COMMON TRAITS OF SUCCESSFUL PEOPLE

"Getting ahead in a difficult profession requires avid faith in yourself. That is why some people with mediocre talent, but with great inner drive, go much further than people with vastly superior talent." -Sophia Loren

When I set out to write this book, I studied a number of successful people to discover their keys to success in hopes of being able to mimic their success. In all honesty, before I ever decided to turn this idea into a book, I studied the lives of successful people. Just so you know, I didn't stalk them, rummage through their trash, or peer through their windows to see what their lives were like; I studied them from afar, like a normal person.

First, it was learning more about my favorite athletes and entertainers, trying to figure out what drove Tiger Woods to be as competitive as he is or what inspired Michael Jackson's musical genius. However, as I began to seek answers to these questions about people I naturally had an interest in, I began to seek out other successful people. Some were people I naturally followed either because I enjoyed their work or had heard a lot about them, while others were successful individuals I was fascinated with and wanted to find out what made them successful. So, in reality, I owe a great deal of the material in this book to all the successful people around the world. On second thought, please ignore that last sentence. My publisher, attorney and common sense have alerted me that this book, its ideas, words, punctuations and pictures were all mine and no one deserves credit for this, not even the people I thanked in the beginning of this book. Just kidding. I actually owe them a lot.

Contrary to popular belief, there is no such thing as "self-made." We are who we are thanks to our family, friends, enemies and experiences. Even though my name appears as the sole author of this book, I owe a great deal of thanks and gratitude to the many people who helped make this possible. Just as these people helped me in my journey to success, my goal is to share my knowledge with you and help guide you on your way to becoming successful in your own way/right.

During my research, one person I studied was Andrew Carnegie. Andrew Carnegie was a Scottish-American industrialist who led the enormous expansion of the American steel industry in the late 19th century to become one of the richest people in world history. In 1908, he commissioned journalist Napoleon Hill to interview more than 500 wealthy achievers to find out the common threads of their success.[3] Carnegie and Hill worked on this project for a number of years and in 1928, after Carnegie's death, their work was published in Hill's famous book entitled *The Law of Success*[4]. Their work was also discussed in Hill's second publication, *Think and Grow Rich*, which was released in 1937. Hill and Carnegie endeavored to learn the common threads of successful people and I undertook the same mission.

The major differences between my work and that of Carnegie and Hill are:

(1) My focus is on developing steps and strategies uniquely tailored for millennials people;

(2) The steps I believe you should take can be universally applied to millennials across varying disciplines, rather than those that fit within a tightly constructed niche that lies in the core subjects; and

(3) I didn't take 28 years to complete the task.

It is my belief and experience that people are largely the same at our core. However, there are variations when we take certain factors into account, factors such as age, gender, race, religion and socioeconomic status. For instance, studies prove that the higher the median wealth in your family, the more likely you are to get a high score on standardized tests such as the SAT/ACT. Yet, my experience has taught me that outside of the classroom, success is relative.

We know that when it comes to a math test there is no dispute between an "A" and an "F". If you receive an "A", it means that you knew the material, or that you have a very impressive memory and were able to exhibit that knowledge in a timely manner in the fashion required by the test giver. We also know that if you receive an "F", it's more likely than not, although no guarantee, that you earned the grade because of your lack of grasp of the material, your failure to follow instructions, or because you fell asleep. But what if you don't want to be a NASA scientist, Rhodes Scholar, or come anywhere near a quadratic equation in your professional career? What if you want to be a professional athlete, an artist, a social worker, a lawyer, a writer, or engage in some other non-math, non-science based profession? Can you not succeed in these endeavors because you didn't do well on a test?

Often times, we equate our knowledge, or lack thereof, of core subjects to intellect, but this is a flawed theory; one that completely devalues and overlooks a very large segment of the population who will never be able to solve for X, but can paint a portrait that contains more than just stick figures, or compose a symphony, or be a high school English teacher. For these people, success looks, feels and sounds much different. So what about them?

Consequently, I've learned to view success as something much broader in scope and more malleable as it pertains to individuals. As a result, I've constructed what I believe to be the most widely applicable steps regardless of whether you want to be a writer or a civil engineer, a professional tennis player or a psychiatrist, a musician or an accountant. Regardless of what career path you take, there are few universal core steps we must all take to be successful; the first step starts with finding out the commonalities of successful people.

Beneath the surface, successful people share at least four commonalities. Yes they are rich, likely famous, probably good looking and did I mention rich? But, those aren't the four commonalities I'm referencing. I'm referring to four common traits that every successful person possesses; four traits that we should mimic if we strive to be successful as well.

One of the common attributes of successful people is that they have all encountered some form of adversity; adversity that stood in the way of their success and adversity that they ultimately overcame to become the successful people they are today. These are people who have used obstacles as stepping stones as opposed to stop signs. Successful people see a problem and, rather than give up on their dreams, they seek to solve the problem and continue the quest. Unlike most people, when successful people reach a stumbling block they view it as a building block for greatness. They take the bricks thrown at them by doubters and use them to build a bridge to success. Why can't we all do that?

We all go through stuff; anyone who tells you different is a witch and should be burned at the stake. Well probably not, but at the very least you shouldn't be taking advice from this person because this person is a liar and the truth isn't in them. Life isn't about the potholes in the road, the random thunderstorms on a clear sunny day, or stepping in poop while wearing new sneakers or open-toe shoes. Life is about what you do once all of that stuff has happened. Do you cry about the rain or do you go outside, play in it and turn the day into a movie day? Whining about what's going on in your life will leave you nowhere but alone because, eventually, the friends you have will avoid you like the plague.

It's okay to complain, just don't sulk or dwell on it. The quicker we're able to assess a situation and move on, the better off we'll be. Sulking and dwelling are the beginning points of sadness, depression and substance abuse which we engage in to help us get over the sadness and depression that got us there in the first place. So what's the point? Honestly, there isn't one. We must focus more on solving the problems at hand rather than wallowing in the muddiness of the situation. When you focus on the solution, then, and only then, can you find the answers you're searching for. So next time you experience hard times, instead of getting sad and depressed, find a way to accept it, deal with it and keep it moving to the next best thing. I promise you, no matter how tough the task at hand may be, it won't last forever, and when it ends you'll be more prepared to handle the next hard assignment.

The second common trait successful people share is that they have the intestinal fortitude of a farm pig. I liken successful people to pigs not as an insult but as a compliment. Pigs have the ability to digest just about anything that they consume. Successful people, like pigs, have an uncanny ability to take whatever comes their way, deal with it and still maintain focus on their ultimate goal. Very few people possess this quality, but intestinal fortitude is one of the best qualities you can have to conquer this thing we call life, or at least be able to eat moldy bread and live to tell about it.

When I was in high school I ran track. I was a middle-distance runner, 800 meters and 1,600 meters mostly. Out of all the events that are run during a track and field competition, not once did it ever occur to me to become a hurdler. There are a number of reasons why: (1) It was way too much work for a person who only ran track to train and condition for football; (2) I wasn't sure my legs were long enough; and (3) See #1. What separates a hurdler from a sprinter is the same thing that separates a successful person from an unsuccessful person, the ability to overcome every hurdle placed in front of him.

Life is not a 100 meter dash. Life is more like a 200,000 meter hurdle race. In this race there will be hurdle after hurdle after hurdle. The key to finishing strong is to find a way to get over every hurdle. It doesn't have to be perfect, it doesn't have to be clean and it doesn't have to be pretty. It just needs to happen. Successful people hurdle every obstacle placed in front of them until they reach the end, which for most successful people is death, but for others, it's the last stage of Call of Duty or getting into a new dress for a wedding or big event. How you choose to handle your hurdles will determine whether you have the intestinal fortitude of a pig or that of an eighty year old man with irritable bowel syndrome. Choose wisely.

The third common trait successful people share is that they have an unwavering belief in themselves, their talents and their abilities. Mahatma Gandhi wrote, "A man is but the product of his thoughts. What he thinks he becomes." In order to be successful you have to believe that you can and will be successful. Those who have experienced success undoubtedly have endured moments of self-doubt. We're humans and it's inevitable. However, when doubt seeps in, successful people are able to defeat it with thoughts of greatness, belief in themselves, their dreams and their abilities.

To a large degree, what happens outside is insignificant compared to what is going on inside. Regardless of what is going on outside on the blogs, in magazines and newspapers, or on social media sites, if you don't believe in yourself, your talent and your ability, it means nothing. People can praise or ridicule you as much as they want, but without a strong belief in yourself none of it matters. Ella Wheeler Wilcox once stated, "It is possible for you to do whatever you choose, if you first get to know who you are and are willing to work with a power that is greater than ourselves to do it." Belief in yourself is an immeasurable power that may lead to countless possibilities, but only if you believe.

The fourth trait that successful people share is their desire and ability to control their environment. I'm not talking about the room temperature, the color of the shades, or making sure the Skittles in the jar of the green room at "The Daily Show" are only red and purple. I mean those things in the environment that they can't control, such as the weather, gossip, and whom their exes marry and date; these are things they cannot do anything about, so they don't worry about them. Those things that they can control, their response to these things, their demeanor, their behavior, and their attitude, they do control. You can't let external forces dictate your internal mood. Once you do, you've lost all control and one thing successful people enjoy is being in control.

The ability to exercise control over the things we can control, not worry about the things we can't control and be wise enough to tell the difference between the two is a character trait successful people share. The ability to not sweat the small stuff and shrug your shoulders at the things beyond our reach is a superhero power we all should hope to fall in a toxic vat of goo to obtain. Learn to focus on the important things in life, let go of the rest and become Captain Unstoppable or Lady Impenetrable.

A lot of information about being successful can be garnered from successful people, more than just their style, where to vacation and how and where to get free stuff. Personally, I subscribe to the theory that there is nothing new under the sun and firmly believe in the idea that there is no need to reinvent the wheel. In other words, we should study the acts, habits and ideas of people who have been successful in the areas that we want to venture into and get to work.

I've even found it helpful to study the lives of successful people in areas I have absolutely no desire to be in or pursue. For instance, there is no bone in my body that longs to be a scientist, doctor, mathematician or work in any field that deals with blood, bones, math, science, or feet. However, examining the work of greats like Albert Einstein, Madam C.J. Walker, Benjamin Franklin and many others has been enlightening and I have learned a great deal from each of these people that has helped me to be successful in my own right.

Ultimately, the key is to figure out what makes those who are successful tick, what drives them and what moves them, and then use those qualities to help you overcome challenges and similar circumstances in your own life. Don't worry, this isn't a quiz or a test so copying their styles isn't cheating. Actually, in this instance, it's perfectly okay to borrow the great ideas of someone else to help yourself become successful. The moral of the story is you should learn how to be successful from other successful people. Who are these people you ask? Well, you're in luck because we will examine a number of successful people and examine their traits, in depth, throughout the rest of this book. As we begin our journey into the 5 steps of becoming a dream maker, let me leave you with this:

"Making your mark on the world is hard. If it were easy, everybody would do it. But it's not. It takes patience, it takes commitment, and it comes with plenty of failure along the way. The real test is not whether you avoid this failure, because you won't. It's whether you let it harden or shame you into inaction, or whether you learn from it; whether you choose to persevere."
-President Barack Obama

CHAPTER 1 REFLECTIONS: COMMONALITIES OF SUCCESSFUL PEOPLE

1. WHAT ARE THE FOUR COMMONALITIES OF SUCCESSFUL PEOPLE?

2. FOR EACH COMMONALITY, STATE WHETHER YOU HAVE THIS TRAIT.

3. FOR EVERY TRAIT THAT YOU DO SHARE WITH SUCCESSFUL PEOPLE PLEASE EXPLAIN HOW/WHY.

4. FOR EVERY TRAIT THAT YOU DON'T SHARE WITH SUCCESSFUL PEOPLE, EXPLAIN WHY NOT AND WHAT YOU NEED TO DO TO HAVE THIS TRAIT.

CHAPTER 2: BELIEVE IN YOURSELF

Believe in yourself! Have faith in your abilities! Without a humble but reasonable confidence in your own powers you cannot be successful or happy. -Norman Vincent Peale

In her novel "A Return to Love" Mary Williamson

wrote:

"Our greatest fear is not that we are inadequate, but that we are powerful beyond measure. It is our light, not our darkness, that frightens us. We ask ourselves, who am I to be brilliant, gorgeous, handsome, talented and fabulous? Actually, who are you not to be?"

In the quote referenced above, author Mary Williamson

addresses the fears many of us have: fear that we're bigger than

our circumstances, socioeconomic status and hometown; fear

that we're larger than the restrictions placed on us by society;

fear "that we are powerful beyond measure." Fear is a common

feeling we all experience at some time or another, but what is

fear? Fear is what you experience while watching a scary movie.

Fear is what you experienced as a kid, and may still experience

as an adult, when the lights go out, the room is dark and you are

all alone. Fear is what you experience the moment before you receive the results of that huge test on Shakespeare that you didn't study for. That is fear.

The dictionary defines fear as "a distressing negative sensation induced by a perceived threat. It is a basic survival mechanism occurring in response to a specific stimulus, such as pain or the threat of danger."[5] Contrary to popular belief, fear is not unique to just you and your "thunder buddy" who are deathly afraid of thunder. Fear is a universal emotion that will illicit one of two responses: (1) an urge to confront it; or (2) an urge to flee from it. This urge to confront or run is also known as the fight-or-flight response.[6] This fight-or-flight response happens every time you encounter a snake, the girl who sits in front of you in math class that you haven't had the nerve to ask out yet, or Mike Tyson in a dark alley.

When confronted with a fearful situation, you can choose to stand, fight and confront the fear of that biology test or asking your crush to prom or you can choose to run. However, be mindful that if you choose to run today, you better head to the nearest shoe store and get yourself a comfortable pair of running shoes because you'll need them since you'll be running for the rest of your life. On the other hand, if you choose to confront your fears, you've won because the first step in overcoming fear is to meet it head on. While that alone won't make your fear of heights, tight spaces, spiders and your Spanish teacher disappear, it is a step in the right direction.

I think that part of the reason millennials all over the world don't do more is because they're scared; yes, you're scared. I think you're scared of being told no, scared of the uncertainty and scared of failure. Your failure to act and do isn't because you're selfish or inconsiderate, and it isn't because you can't help; it's because you're afraid of what awaits you on the other side of the risk you must take when you choose to follow your dreams. Bill Cosby once said, "In order to succeed, your desire for success should be greater than your fear of failure." If you let your fear of failure and the unknown consume you, you will never experience success. That is why the first step on the path to success is so important, because it involves taking a risk; while you might fail, which is terrifying to say the least, taking the risk is necessary. You should never be afraid to give up the good to go for the great.

If successful people succumbed to failure, they wouldn't be successful and we may not have light bulbs and airplanes because people would have been too afraid to invent them. In Thomas Edison's early years, his teachers told him he was "too stupid to learn anything" and he was fired from his first two jobs for not being productive enough. However, that didn't stop him. Edison went on to make more than a thousand unsuccessful attempts at inventing the light bulb before he got it right. In regards to his many failed attempts to create the light bulb, Edison remarked, "I have not failed. I've just found 10,000 ways that won't work." That's a powerful lesson.

Another example of taking a risk with persistence and fortitude are the Wright brothers. Brothers Orville and Wilbur Wright both battled depression and family illness before starting the bicycle shop that led them to experiment with flight. After numerous attempts at creating flying machines, several years of hard work, and tons of failed prototypes, the Wright Brothers finally created a plane that could get airborne and stay there. Today, they are known as the pioneers of flight. Could you imagine living in a world with no light bulbs or airplanes? I, for one, am thankful they had the courage to pursue their dreams into the dark places where they led and were confident that if they worked hard enough, and long enough, the light would eventually come on (pun intended).

Neither Edison nor the Wright Brothers folded under pressure or surrendered to failure; instead, they kept trying until they were successful. Both successful and unsuccessful people alike have encountered fear and disappointment at many turns. However, the difference between the two is that instead of turning and running, successful people confront their fears and failures, fight them and continue to follow their dreams until they've won.

Every great feat in life begins with a dream. A dream that you can dunk a basketball jumping from the free throw line; a dream that one day the captain of the football team will notice you and not just because you have toilet paper stuck to your shoe; a dream that one day you'll be able to sneak in the house without your parents noticing; and a dream that one day you'll be the first person in your family to attend and graduate from college. The dream serves as the vision, the starting point and the catalyst to get what we want. It's the gas the engine needs to work. It's the steam the locomotive needs to move. It's the sunlight and water plants need to grow. Yet, in order to power this dream and turn it into reality, you have to believe in yourself.

The story behind one of the greatest basketball players to ever lace up a pair of sneakers involves believing in yourself. I grew up in the 90's watching the Chicago Bulls dominate basketball. My favorite player on the team, and one of my favorite athletes of all time, was Michael Jordan. I admire the way he seemed to fly through the air, the way he could get his shot off whenever he wanted and the suffocating defense he would apply at a moment's notice. I also liked his cockiness, tenacity, determination and work ethic.

It was no secret that Michael Jordan was one of the hardest working athletes in the world. Yes, he was blessed with the ability of flight; however, he knew that he couldn't out-jump everyone. As such, he developed a jump shot, the ability to fade away from both sides and the skill to negotiate his shot in traffic. It was this initial infatuation with my childhood hero that led me to delve deeper into his life to see if it was "really the shoes" the way the Nike commercials said it was, or if it was something else. My decision to explore what made him successful led me to the discovery of little-known facts about his life that inevitably steered him to becoming a champion.

Before Michael Jordan became "Air Jordan", he was a little boy growing up in Wilmington, North Carolina. He was a three-sport athlete who played football, baseball and basketball. However, basketball was where he excelled the most. During his sophomore year of high school, Jordan tried out for the varsity basketball team. At 5'11", he was told that he wasn't tall enough to play and was denied a spot on the varsity team. That year, Jordan settled for playing on the junior varsity team where he tallied several forty point games.

Based on his great JV performance, the following season they couldn't deny him a varsity roster spot. However, before he got his opportunity to play on the varsity team he had a choice; he could choose to accept what the coaches and other players thought of him and his talent during his sophomore year or he could choose to believe in himself and prove them wrong. He chose the latter and made the varsity basketball team the next season. He later went on to win a college national championship, two Olympic gold medals, three NBA All Star game MVP titles, five Most Valuable Player Awards, six NBA Championships, a bust in the NBA Hall of Fame, and many other awards and accolades.

Yet, before Michael Jordan won all of those awards, before he became the richest man in sports, and before he became the world's greatest basketball player of all time, he had a dream. When the coaches and other players didn't believe in him, he believed in himself. We can learn a lot from Michael Jordan. His story proves that we can't rely on other people to improve our self-esteem. It's impossible. It's called self-esteem, esteem of one's self. Therefore, the only person in control of it is you; so if you don't believe in you, no one else will.

I know first-hand about the power of self-esteem and believing in yourself. I have three brothers and one sister and I'm the second youngest of five. My brother who immediately precedes me in age, Chris, is seven years older than me. When I was younger I always wanted to do everything he did. Needless to say, much of the things he did and many of the places he went, I couldn't do or go. After all, he was seven years older than me. However, one of the things I never let him or my parents stop me from doing was playing sports with him, especially football. I'm from Florida where football is king, so my siblings and I worshipped football much like everyone else.

My brother was a pretty good athlete with a cannon for an arm. Whenever we played around the neighborhood he was almost always quarterback. He was so good that if it was a small game, he would play quarterback for both teams. Unfortunately, as great as Chris was at playing quarterback, there were a few things that kept him from being a major standout player at the position: (1) His height (At 6 feet tall he was kind of short for a quarterback); (2) The local high school football team was led by legendary football coach Walt Frazier who ran an offensive system contrary to what Chris wanted to do, which was air it out; and (3) The team had a quarterback who was Mr. Football in the state of Florida and who was awarded a full scholarship to play Division I football at the University of Miami. Absent those things my big brother would have been a great quarterback and I wanted to learn from and play ball with him.

One day, I conjured up the nerve to ask Chris if I could play with the big boys. Surprisingly, he didn't outright say "no" (or maybe he did and I just don't remember it that way). What I do remember him saying is that if I played with the older guys, he wouldn't tell them to take it easy on me and he wouldn't protect me. He told me there was no way he could play and referee at the same time; or maybe he could and just didn't want to. Anyway, whatever the reason, it didn't take me more than a moment to jump at the opportunity.

You see, despite the fact that I was shorter and smaller than most of the other players on the field, I believed that I could play with them. It also helped that I was just as fast as them, if not faster, and was smart enough to run out of bounds at the sight of some of the bigger kids in the neighborhood. I knew there was a possibility that I could get hurt, but I believed I could do it; so I played with the big boys. My belief in my ability superseded my fear of injury. That day, I scored two touchdowns playing against guys I should have never gained a yard against. After that game,

I joined my high school football team where I earned a couple of varsity letters. Later on, I played in college where I earned All-Conference honors my freshman year. If you ask me, it was my belief in me and my ability that day playing sandlot football that ignited my success.

Michael Jordan's belief in himself sparked his success, much like I believe my confidence in myself sparked mine. Grant it, comparatively speaking, MJ's success was much greater than mine in the sports arena, but he's MJ. Most people's accomplishments in athletics pale in comparison to his, so I'm okay with that. Besides, I found out a while ago that while I could play football very well, football was not my calling.

My calling is touching the lives of those who I come in contact with, sharing words of inspiration and little known facts about things you don't even know you care about. We all have different callings on our lives, missions, skills and talents that we are purposed to cultivate and share with the world. No matter what your calling is, whether it is science, math, athletics, writing, music or something else, fulfilling the purpose on your life starts with you believing in yourself.

"Believe you can and you're halfway there."
–Theodore Roosevelt

CHAPTER 2 REFLECTIONS: STEP 1- BELIEVE IN YOURSELF

1. DO YOU BELIEVE IN YOURSELF?

2. WHAT DOES BELIEVING IN YOURSELF MEAN TO YOU?

3. WHY OR WHY NOT?

4. WHY IS BELIEVING IN YOURSELF IMPORTANT TO FOLLOWING YOUR DREAMS?

CHAPTER 3: STEP 2-MAKE A PLAN

"The first step to getting the things you want out of life is this: decide what you want." -Ben Stein

Road trips are fun. Well they can be depending on whom you go with, where you go, how long it takes you to get there, whether you have snacks, a good "road trip playlist", and provided that you know where you're going. I imagine a convicted felon's road trip to state prison probably doesn't fit the above description. But, if you're a college student heading to spring break in Daytona with some friends, or a couple taking a romantic weekend getaway to the Poconos, or a kid in the car with your family on the way to Disney, there is great potential for the trip to be epic. However, there is also equally as great a potential for the trip to go down in the Guinness Book of World Records as "The Worst Trip Ever Known to Man."

To avoid having a colossal failure of a trip, before you hit the road you have to first decide where you want to go and determine how to get there. You can't go to Disney if you don't know that you're going to Disney because it's nearly impossible to reach a destination that you haven't decided to go to. So, you have to figure out the destination first. After you've decided where you want to go you then have to figure out how to get there. With everything in life we must have a plan. If we fail to plan, then we plan to fail.

Successful people plan to be successful. Professional sports feature competition that pits the fastest, strongest and most athletic people in the world against each other to engage in competition. Often times, it's not the athletes alone that determine the outcomes of the competitions, it's the game plan; the strategy on how to beat the opponent, and the execution of said game plan, determines the outcome of the competition.

While it's great to assemble a team with the world's greatest athletes, put them out there and tell them to just play, we've seen incidences where this doesn't work (2004 Men's Olympic Basketball Team, 2011-2012 Philadelphia Eagles, 2010-2011 Miami Heat, and every Yankees team in recent history that hasn't won the World Series, just to name a few). Yes, it helps to have a good coach to get the most out of the team, to get them to play together, and to help them stick to the plan, but it's often not enough to be smart, fast, or really strong.

To increase the likelihood of success, you have to combine your talent and ability with a good game plan, a roadmap and a projected path to success. As you set out on your quest for success, you will expect certain results because expectations are a part of life.

Every accomplishment is coupled with expectations; not just normal, regular expectations, but lofty, high expectations. For example, once Jay Z's first album went platinum people expected every album he made to sell over a million copies. When Kobe Bryant hit his first game winning shot, people expected him to hit them all. Even for champions, the first championship is the hardest to win until you try to win your second and that's due, in part, to the grandiose expectations that follow the first victory.

Winning is tough and a part of that is dealing with the expectations. Despite the star quality of the individuals associated with these expectations, the expectations are still pretty high. In life, what we must realize is that high and often unreasonable expectations are as unavoidable as death and taxes. Live long enough and you'll have to deal with all three of these.

However, having a good plan will help you deal with death, taxes and the high expectations.

When I was younger, I grappled with the expectations placed on me by others and struggled with how to manage them. When I was in middle school I was placed in the gifted program. The gifted program is for students who are said to be "really smart." I liked the title of "gifted" and the idea of being smarter than my classmates, but I didn't like the pressure that came along with it.

For me, as a middle school kid, it was tough, but I wasn't the only one who struggled. I had a class full of classmates who felt the strain and burden of the title, much like I did, and because we didn't know how to handle it, we rebelled. And when I say we rebelled, I mean rebelled like the South against the North in the Civil War. I'm talking *Game of Thrones* level of uprisings. We fought our label the way your stomach fought against you after you ate that expired yogurt during an epic session of truth or dare.

The only difference between us and the truly dysfunctional kids was that we could read and write better; aside from that, there really was no difference. We made teachers and students cry, we made a teacher quit and we may have even led one to have a heart attack (although for legal purposes, I will neither confirm nor deny this). I was so bad I can count on one hand the number of fieldtrips I was allowed to go on in the three years I was there. In fact, I was so much of a problem child that I almost failed the 6th, 7th and 8th grades. Were it not for two very special people, Mr. Litman my math teacher and Ms. Altman the gifted Language Arts teacher, I would have failed miserably; however, they had a plan for me and were invested in my success even when I had no plan and no interest in finding my own.

My father also had a plan and he got me on track. Eventually, he got sick and tired. He got sick and tired of hearing how terrible his son was; he got sick and tired of the embarrassment and shame I brought to him and my mother, and he got sick and tired of me thinking that I could do what I wanted, when I wanted. So, to fix my behavior, he told me that I couldn't play high school football the following year. At that moment, he could have stuck his hand in my chest and ripped out my heart, like a Mortal Kombat finishing move, which would have caused me less pain than he did the moment he uttered those words. But, I realized I had a choice. I had an option to continue to rebel or to straighten up and fly right. Football was my passion, my love, and my life, so not playing ball was like not breathing. Since football and breathing were such an integral part of my life, I had to come up with a plan to get out on that field.

My first plan was to beg and plead and hope that would work. It didn't. My father was a hard man to budge and I'm not just saying that because he's 6'3" and 250 pounds. I say that because he is as stubborn as a mule (a character trait I inherited) and once he makes a ruling on something, there isn't anyone or anything short of Jesus and a miracle that can change his mind; and this time, I was all out of prayers and holy water.

When that didn't work I had to go to plan B. This plan was to raise my grades, be respectful to my teachers, stay out of trouble and return to an oldie but a goodie…begging and pleading. While I'm sure my plan was pretty solid, I never persuaded my father to let me play football my freshman year of high school. That year I learned a painful lesson. However, were it not for that lesson, I wouldn't have learned the importance of doing the right thing, making a plan and sticking to it. I am certain that if I had backed out of the plan before its completion, my father would have buried me in the back yard next to the dog and I still would have been stuck not playing football.

Although I didn't get to play football in 9th grade, I did however play my 10th grade year so my plan worked. By the time I graduated from high school, I had won more trophies, certificates, plaques and scholarships than my parents had room enough to house AND I got to play football. You see, I took that plan to play football and used it to help me get through high school as a successful student and athlete; I won because I had a plan and so can you.

"Setting goals is the first step in turning the invisible into the visible." **-Tony Robbins**

CHAPTER 3 REFLECTIONS: STEP 2-MAKE A PLAN

1. WHAT IS YOUR PLAN TO BE SUCCESSFUL?

2. WHAT IS YOUR 5 YEAR PLAN?

3. WHAT IS YOUR 10 YEAR PLAN?

4. WHAT DO YOU NEED TO DO MAKE THESE PLANS HAPPEN?

CHAPTER 4: STEP 3- JUST DO IT!

"Just Do It!" -Nike

Nike is the Greek goddess of victory and the inspiration for the name of a major manufacturer of sports equipment that is also the world's leading supplier of athletic shoes and apparel, Nike, Inc. Nike employs more than 35,000 people across six continents and in fiscal year 2012, they made record-breaking profits totaling more than $24.1 billion[7].

One of Nike's most enduring trademarks, aside from the swoosh logo, is its slogan "Just Do It." Dan Wieden, the co-founder of the Portland-based advertising company Wieden & Kennedy, coined the now-famous slogan *"Just Do It"* for a 1988 Nike ad campaign. This phrase was chosen by *Advertising Age* as one of the top five ad slogans of the 20th century, and the campaign has been enshrined in the Smithsonian Institution. Wieden credits Gary Gilmore as his inspiration for the famous Nike slogan. Gilmore, an infamous criminal, uttered the words "Let's do it" as the last words he spoke before he was executed.

Who knew these words would lead to the creation of one of the most popular slogans in the world.[8]

The iconic phrase "Just Do It" is captivating for a number of reasons. First of all, the athletes who represent this slogan, LeBron James, Sanya Richards-Ross, Calvin Johnson, Hope Solo, Roger Federer, Derek Jeter and Tiger Woods, just to name a few, are some of the best in the world in their respective sports. If you look past the iconic sports heroes and their multi-million dollar ad campaigns, you'll see more. You'll see a decree to put aside your fears and timidity and simply, "Just do it." This slogan, paired with creative advertising, tells us that if the athletes in the commercials can do it, so can we. The ads directly focus on the athletes by emphasizing their drive, will and determination to succeed. The ads show that they didn't do it with fancy equipment, technology, by accident, or magic. They did it by working harder than anyone else and longer than anyone else, to become better athletes than everyone else.

There have been many times in my life where I've been faced with the choice of whether to sit back or "Just do it." Before deciding to write this book I served as the Lead Teacher and Director of the Center for Legal and Public Affairs Magnet Program at Miami Carol City Senior High School. I know what you're thinking, "why would an attorney teach high school when he could be making tons of money practicing law?" Well, let me explain. First of all, there are a lot of things wrong with that question, one of them being the assumption that most attorneys are filthy rich and buy out the bar at the club every weekend.

The most successful attorneys are rich but not wealthy. The difference between the two levels is that if you're rich, you enjoy a comfortable lifestyle based on the income that you generate from working regularly. Basically, you work for your money and you make lots of it; however, if you stopped working for a prolonged period of time, absent a retirement fund, social security and a good savings plan, you couldn't reasonably maintain the lifestyle you had while you were working fulltime.

Whereas wealthy people enjoy an even more lavish lifestyle, in part, because they have more money and don't necessarily have to "work" for it. Their money works for them and if they decided they no longer wanted to show up at an office, go to a board meeting, or punch another clock, (see Bill

Gates, Mitt Romney and Warren Buffett) they would still be set for life. As long as they don't go to Las Vegas and bet their entire net worth on one hand of blackjack, they will always have a lot of money. The moral of the story is this: all attorneys aren't rich. However, the true answer to your question regarding why I put my practice of law in the backseat to take over a struggling law and criminal justice magnet program is pretty complex.

I'm a family man, always have been and always will be. When I graduated from Howard University School of Law, affectionately called the HUSL, I moved to Chicago to take a position as an Assistant State's Attorney at the Cook County State's Attorney's Office. The Cook County State's Attorney's Office is the second largest prosecutor's office in the country and one of the most prestigious offices in the United States, so I was lucky to work there. For me, a person who knew at an early age that I wanted to be a litigator -- the next Robert Shapiro, Johnny Cochran, or Willie Gary -- having the opportunity to work for a prosecutor's office with the promise of early trial experience was a dream come true.

Unfortunately, almost a year into my tenure at the State's Attorney's Office, I got word from home that my grandmother, on my mother's side, was gravely ill and was growing weaker by the day. My mother was tasked with most of the day-to-day duties of caring for her, but given my grandmother's needs this was too much for one person. At this particular time in my life, between college, law school and my time in Chicago, I had been away from home for approximately eight years, so I was used to being away from my family. I always dreamed of coming home to eventually practice and be closer to my family but not so soon, and definitely not under those circumstances. However, given my grandmother's prognosis and her growing needs, it became abundantly clear what I needed to do. I needed to go home, help out and be close to my family. After making this tough decision, I formulated a plan and got to work.

I made a phone call to a long-time friend, just to catch up and let her know my intentions of coming home, and she suggested that I take over the magnet program at my alma mater. Of course, I scoffed at the mere thought of such a thing. It's not that I had never thought about it. In fact, it was something that I wanted to do, after I retired, but not this early in my career. I was a young attorney and I wanted to practice. However, the more I thought about the opportunity the more I thought it was a good fit. The students would have a young, "experienced" and vested attorney to serve as their leader. It would be an opportunity for me to give back to my community, be close to my family and friends and add something different to my resume; it was a win-win situation. Additionally, at most, it was a 2 to 3 year stop so I decided to "Just do it!"

During those two years, I missed practicing law full-time but, given the flexible scheduling of the school calendar, I still got to do a few law-related things. Even looking back now, given everything I learned from and about the educational system, my co-workers, the experience and the students, taking the position was definitely the right decision.

As an educator, I encountered hundreds of kids every day. However, long before I decided to accept the position, on numerous occasions I heard friends and colleagues say that "kids these days just aren't the same." I had heard this statement time and time again about my generation, the generation after mine and I'm sure that if I live long enough to witness future generations, I'll hear it plenty more. Consequently, I ignored the warnings, choosing instead to assess the situation myself and reach my own conclusions about just how different these students were from students of the past.

Going to work every day, walking the halls of a senior high school, listening to their conversations, observing their behavior and trying to mold these young minds was an eye opening experience, to say the least. During that time, I learned several things: (1) a mind truly is a terrible thing to waste; (2) teaching is a lot harder than I thought it was; (3) I look young enough to be mistaken for a student; and (4) my friends and fellow teachers were right—kids these days are different from how I remember them. I have witnessed the lack of initiative, drive, motivation, and sense of urgency that consumes this generation. Some youth walk around so blinded by what's going on today, they can't see that tomorrow is just on the horizon.

Many of you are so preoccupied with your iPods, Mohawks, hair-do's and the latest dance moves, you fail to see that the future is rapidly approaching and that you're vastly unprepared. Today, so many young people are wrapped up in their G-Shocks and Nikes, Polo and American Eagle, Drake and Nicki Minaj that they fail to see that in the blink of an eye, it will all be over. There is absolutely, positively nothing wrong with having fun. I encourage you to have as much as fun as you can possibly squeeze out of life. However, there is a time and a place for everything and you should choose to do the things you don't need to do today, so you can live the life you want to live tomorrow.

I believe the world's greatest assets are youth and young adults; you. It is you whom marketing executives target the most. It is you, those over the age of 18, political candidates and strategists identify as having a significant and key impact on elections. It is you who can bring about the change so many people desperately talk about and hope for. It's not enough to have potential; you must recognize it and use it as well. Realize your power and use it to help change the world.

The greatest movements in the world have all had youth and young adults at their center. The fight for equal rights is an example of youth being at the center of a dynamic movement. After the signing of the Emancipation Proclamation in 1863, a decree that freed the slaves in the South, the conclusion of the Civil War in 1865, and the passing of the Thirteenth (1865), Fourteenth (1868) and Fifteenth Amendments (1870) ("The Reconstruction Amendments"), there was a struggle for Blacks to gain rights equal to those of their Caucasian counterparts. Blacks fought for equality in the face of prejudice, racism and Jim Crow laws, laws that essentially legalized racial separation and permitted disparate treatment.

Black people had serious problems. We were being treated as less than human. We were forced to order food from the back of white-owned restaurants, ride in the back of buses and give up our seats if a white person didn't have one close to the front. We were beaten, lynched and killed for little to nothing or just because of the color of our skin. As a result, Black people, as a group, had to figure out how to gain equal "civil rights." We knew we had to be seen, be heard and be organized, but the questions that still remained were, "Who would lead the movement?" Who would stand up, fight, and subject themselves to the abuse? Who would step up for what was right and risk their lives and the safety of their families for equality? Who would take charge and do what was right, no matter the cost, for equal rights?

These questions were posed to older pastors, leaders, teachers, and professors, but none of them spoke up. Who answered the call? A young Black preacher named Rev. Dr. Martin Luther King, Jr. He was reluctant at first, fearful that he wasn't old enough or capable enough to handle the job. He was scared about what this decision might mean for him and his family. He was scared that he might fail, given the enormity of the task. But eventually, Dr. King decided that if no one else would lead the movement, he would and he eventually decided to "Just do it!"

Dr. King was just twenty-six years old when he led the 1955 Montgomery Bus Boycott in response to Rosa Parks' arrest for refusing to give up her bus seat to a white man at the end of a long day of work. Two years later, in 1957, Dr. King helped found the Southern Christian Leadership Conference (SCLC) and served as its first president until his death in 1968. Dr.

King's efforts then led to the 1963 March on Washington where he delivered his famous "I Have a Dream" speech. This speech, delivered to tens of thousands of people, highlighted King's dreams of a nation where racial segregation and inequality were no longer a norm and where his kids could play with kids of all colors and races. The speech highlighted his dream of a society where men would be judged by the content of their character and not by the color of their skin. It was a powerful speech and it truly solidified Dr. King's place at the center of the movement, but he was only 34 years old when he delivered it.

Dr. King led a movement that saw him beaten, jailed, talked about, lied on and deserted. His house was bombed, his family was threatened and he was ultimately assassinated on April 4, 1968 in Memphis, Tennessee because of the stand he took against racial injustice, poverty and his belief in equality and civil rights for all. Yet, before he died and before he left this earth, his hard work, his faith, his determination, his passion and his zeal for this cause paid off in two major ways: (1) He was instrumental in getting the Civil Rights Act of 1964 passed; and (2) In 1964, Dr. King became the youngest person to receive the

Nobel Peace Prize for his work to end racial segregation and racial discrimination through civil disobedience and other nonviolent means.

As a result of his efforts, Blacks, Hispanics and other minorities, like myself, can eat where we want, sleep where we want and sit anywhere on the bus we want. This is all because a young person decided that sitting down and doing nothing was just not enough for him; because a young person decided that he couldn't turn a blind eye to injustice; because a young person got tired of hearing people say "Why me?" and instead asked the question "Why not me?" Because a young person decided to "Just Do It", he helped change the world.

While millennials are the world's greatest assets, you are also like Jay-Z's chart topping album The Blueprint 2, a "Gift and a Curse". The gifts you bring are your large numbers, drive, passion, youth and energy. When millennials support something they believe in: Drake, Rick Ross, Madden, Nike, the products sell and do well. However, some millennials are cursed with a lack of ambition and motivation, a sense of complacency and a sense of entitlement. Somewhere along the way, someone told them that they were smart, halfway cute and hotter than a Florida highway in the middle of July and it went to their heads.

Be mindful young people that you're never as smart as you think you are, beauty fades and that we should always strive to learn something new. George Bernard Shaw once said, "Youth is wasted on the young." This is because by the time you are old enough to know what to do with your time and energy you don't have much left of either. My suggestion: do something with the time and energy you have while you still have it. Every day is an opportunity to do better and be better than the day before. Don't waste your opportunity because you don't know when the next one will be your last.

Don't ever think that you're too young to make a difference or to effect change. It was young people that helped elect Barack Obama, the nation's first Black president. It was the young adults who hit the streets telling the country about Barack Hussein Obama, then just a freshman Senator from Illinois. It was young adults who helped him raise the millions of dollars they said he couldn't raise. It was young adults who helped him make history in 2008 and it was young adults who he counted on to help him make history again in 2012. You can do anything you put your mind to because hard work knows no bounds, but you must first believe.

The rapper Drake may have said it best in his song aptly entitled "The Motto," where he proclaims "You only live once that's the motto [ ] Y.O.L.O." I believe we should adopt Drake's motto to live life to the fullest. However, we should also be mindful that the concept of "Y.O.L.O." isn't to go smoke, drink, and live life recklessly. Rather, it's to go out and do something with your life that matters. We have to get up from the Xbox1 and the PS4 and make a change. We have to take our iPods out of our ears, or at least turn the volume down, and make a change. We need to be the change we want to see in the world because if we wait around for someone else to do it we may be waiting forever.

Whether you're a varsity athlete, casual observer, weekend warrior, or couch potato, there comes a time in each and every one of our lives where we have to decide whether or not we will "Just Do It!" The choices we make at these pivotal moments will shape and define us. Will you choose to seize the moment or will you choose to sit and watch life pass you by? Will you take full advantage of every opportunity presented to you to be successful and follow your dreams or will you take the easy way out and sit on the sidelines? The choice is yours but my advice: choose to "Just Do It!"

"All our dreams can come true, if we have the courage to pursue them." –**Walt Disney**

CHAPTER 4 REFLECTIONS: STEP 3- JUST DO IT!

1. WHAT ARE SOME OF THE THINGS YOU WANT TO "JUST DO"?

2. HAVE YOU "JUST DONE IT" YET? IF NOT, WHAT'S STOPPING YOU?

3. WHAT DOES "JUST DO IT" MEAN FOR YOU AND YOUR PLAN TO MAKE YOUR DREAMS COME TRUE?

4. WHAT STANDS IN THE WAY OF YOU MAKING YOUR DREAMS COME TRUE?

5. WHAT DO YOU NEED TO DO TO OVERCOME WHAT'S STANDING IN YOUR WAY?

CHAPTER 5: STEP 4- PUSH THROUGH THE PAIN

"The ultimate measure of a man is not where he stands in moments of comfort and convenience, but where he stands at times of challenge and controversy."-Martin Luther King, Jr.

Before a car leaves the manufacturer, it is put through rigorous tests and challenges to ensure that it is prepared to handle the day-to-day needs of the average driver. The vehicle is road tested in extreme conditions and situations, many of which the vehicle is unlikely to experience in the real world with the average driver. However, the manufacturer knows that if the vehicle can handle these extreme tests, it can handle anything. This process is much like our life experience.

Life is a constant test. In order to make it to the next big thing, you have to overcome the big thing presently in front of you. By no stretch of the imagination is being 16 easy, but it's at least bearable because of the 15 years of life you experienced before you turned 16. As much as I enjoyed my experiences in law school, law school sucked; but it helped me become the man I am today. Everything that I am and everything that I've accomplished has been born out of strife. When I think about it, my best moments have come when my world was at its darkest and my light at its dimmest.

Growing up I only wanted to do one of two things, play professional football or be a lawyer. Truthfully, football was my plan A. I played in high school and did well; I was even good enough to play in college. Unfortunately, I suffered a significant injury in pre-season camp which put me out for the remainder of camp and a significant portion of the beginning of the season. After a while, I began to notice that I was being looked at and treated differently by some of my teammates and even some of the coaches. I got questions about when I would be back on the field and whether I wanted to be back. At the time I had never experienced such a significant injury in my life, so when it happened I was devastated. On top of that, my teammates and coaches were questioning my passion and desire to play, and that really did something to me. It forced me to man up and push through the pain.

When I was finally able to get back on the field, I felt as if I had played well enough to garner more playing time; however, the coaches saw it differently. Whenever I got the opportunity to play, I ran like I was angry. I was angry like a fat kid on a diet. I was angry like a bear prematurely awakened from hibernation. I was angry like a parent who comes home to find a hole in the wall, crudely patched with a cereal box and paint (sorry mom and dad). After my anger subsided and I was able to think clearly, I realized that the best thing for me to do was to stop playing football and move on.

When the season was over I decided to transfer to another university, focus on Plan B   and no longer pursue football. I still loved football and I always will. However, football was no longer fun for me so I needed a change. I'm thankful for the teammates, friends and experiences I gained during my freshman year of college and I have no regrets. After all, it helped me realize my true calling. When football didn't work out, I knew I had a pretty good back up plan with my desire to be a lawyer. So once I transferred to Florida State University my focus, from day one, was getting to law school.

My passion and drive to make it to law school was no more evident than in my last semester of college. In the early spring of my final semester at Florida State I learned that I had been granted admission into several law schools, one of which was Howard University. Although I got into a lot of schools, Howard was the only school on my top three list to outright accept me, so that's where I decided to go. One school wait-listed me and the other denied me (thanks Florida State). However, with the acceptance letter came a request for a $500 seat deposit needed to guarantee my spot in the incoming class. Unfortunately, this deposit was due before the end of my final undergrad semester and I didn't have it. While I did have an on-campus job, by my math, it wouldn't pay me enough to pay the bills and make the deposit by the deadline. Asking my parents for the money wasn't an option, and neither was selling drugs, panhandling, or selling chicken dinners. So instead, I picked up another job to make sure my seat deposit was paid on time.

My primary job was serving as the Assistant Director of Off-Campus Housing at Florida State. My second, non-paying job was interning with the Florida House of Representatives for State Representative Yolly Roberson in the House Minority Internship Program. This was a wonderful opportunity and I thoroughly enjoyed it. However, by the time I received the invitation to attend Howard, this unpaid opportunity wasn't as glamorous as it used to be. So, I began to ask around and look for paid opportunities. Thanks to the help of the internship coordinator, I was able to secure an interview with Public Affairs Consultants and eventually got the job. For the rest of the semester, in addition to attending classes, club meetings, events, interning and being a senior, I worked two jobs to ensure that I could pay my seat deposit to attend Howard Law. It was tough, but I managed to get my seat deposit paid in time to guarantee my spot in the incoming class. I was headed to law school!

When I first stepped foot on the campus of the Howard University School of Law I thought I had arrived. I knew it would be tough and I knew I would have to work hard, but I had no fear and there was no doubt that I would be the best. School had always come easy to me and this is what I wanted more than anything; I wanted to be an attorney, so I was ready and up to the challenge. Not to mention, based on the work I had put in just to pay my seat deposit, failure was not an option; or so I thought.

My incoming class had one hundred fifty students and we were divided into three sections. It was rumored that my section, Section Two, had been hand-picked from the best and brightest of the class. So to be in that section was a remarkable feat. To this day, there has never been any confirmation that this was in fact the case, but an unsubstantiated rumor is good enough for me. During orientation, we were informed that not everyone seated in the auditorium would finish with us. We were told that not everyone would make it to the finish line and we were encouraged not to be the one who didn't make it. We were also told that the bottom 10% of each class (roughly five students per section) would be placed on academic probation and forced to take a remedial class to pull up their grades; if they failed to do so, they would be kicked out of school.

In my mind none of this applied to me because, as I stated earlier, the rules don't apply to me, so I ignored these words. Also, I've always believed that I can do anything I want to do. Not in the sense that I can speed through red lights and stop signs or commit random assaults, but in the sense that just because someone else can't do something, doesn't mean that I can't either. I pride myself on doing what many find to be hard or impossible no matter how tall the task.

After hearing these warnings, my classmates and I took turns guessing who we thought would be in the "Bottom 5" of our class. Imagine my surprise when some of the students we thought would be at the bottom were not there. Imagine how much more surprised I was when I ended up in the "Bottom 5." Me, of all people?! My world was rocked and even though the names and identities of those in the "Bottom 5" were only known to those in the special class and the professor who taught it, I was ashamed, I was embarrassed, and I was terrified. I had come so far from the terror I was in middle school. I had come so far from the kid from Carol City to a student at one of the best law schools in the country. I had come too far to fail and it appeared, at least at that moment in time, that I would indeed fail.

The following semester I was forced to take an extra class, buy an extra book and do extra work for a class that wouldn't count towards graduation. I didn't tell any of my friends so I was often forced to make up excuses as to why I couldn't meet or hang out with them. However, after getting over the initial shame, I pulled it together, worked hard and successfully made it out. I graduated from Howard with a B average and went on to be a prosecutor at the 2nd largest prosecutor's office in the country. I owe a large portion of my success to Professor Robert Fabrikant, the professor of the class I called the "Don't Drop out of Howard Class", and to my experiences as a member of that class. Were it not for that bout with adversity who knows where I would be today. My time in law school made me realize that adversity really does build character and I'm a better person for it.

My entire life I have tried to pattern my life after successful people I admire and look for similarities between their lives and my own. I tried to match Michael Jordan's jump shot, Bo Jackson's speed and power, Ken Griffey, Jr.'s swing and Michael Jackson's dance moves. Yet, no matter how hard I tried, I just couldn't mirror their shot, speed, power, or their swing and I definitely could not perfect Michael Jackson's lean from "Smooth Criminal" without coming up short (or falling flat on my face). However, my law school experience finally allowed me to share a similarity with Jordan, Jackson, Griffey, Jr. and Jackson; one that I hadn't been looking for, but one that I needed the most: dealing with and overcoming adversity so that you can succeed despite the struggles.

From that experience, I learned that greatness lies in overcoming obstacles. Like LeBron James, Sean "Diddy" Combs, Tyler Perry and Oprah Winfrey, I realized that were it not for that moment, and others like it, I wouldn't be who I am today. What I thought was a mistake or an accident, I later learned was a blessing. Elizabeth Kubler-Ross once said, "There are no mistakes, no coincidences. All events are blessings given to us to learn from." For me, being in the "Bottom Five" was my blessing, even though, in that moment I felt like I had failed and thought it was an embarrassing, shameful mistake.

As I've grown older, I find it fascinating that mistakes can turn out to be the pathway to some of the best moments in your life. For example, many people felt that LeBron James made a huge mistake when he decided to leave Cleveland for Miami; and for those who didn't see it as a mistake, at the very least, they thought he made a mistake in how he left Cleveland with an hour long televised special called "The Decision." In actuality, leaving Cleveland was LeBron's best career move because it resulted in him winning two NBA Championships. Clearly, what some viewed as a mistake was LeBron's blessing because he is now a 2-time champion who will go down in history as one of the greatest NBA players of all time.

Regardless of how you may feel about him as a person, LeBron James is a talented player. At 6'8" and 250 pounds, with a 40-inch vertical and a sub 4.5 second forty yard dash time, he is a physically gifted freak of nature. As a result of his physical tools, in middle school and high school, he was a man among men and the game of basketball was easy for him. Yes, he put in many hours practicing at the gym, both alone and with teammates, but his talent and ability placed him head and shoulders above most of his peers. This was evidenced by his unprecedented receipt of three Mr. Ohio Basketball Awards, his selection to the USA Today All-USA First Team, his being named Gatorade National Player of the Year and his selection to the McDonald's All-American team his senior season. These accolades culminated in James being drafted number one overall by the Cleveland Cavaliers in the 2003 NBA Draft directly out of high school.

However, James' accomplishments did not end after his entrance into the "big leagues," in some ways they were just beginning. In his first NBA season, he received NBA Rookie of the Year honors. He then went on to become a bronze and gold medalist at the Summer Olympics, a ten-time NBA-All Star, a two-time NBA All-Star MVP, and a four-time NBA Most Valuable Player. While he had all of these awards, the one thing that eluded James the most was the NBA Championship trophy.

Prior to the 2011-2012 season, LeBron had twice experienced the bitter taste of defeat in the NBA Finals. Twice he had the game's greatest prize in sight and twice it had escaped his grasp. After coming up short in the finals, there were questions about LeBron's ability to close. He was questioned about whether he had the mental wherewithal to lead a team to the "Promised Land" and if he possessed the so-called "clutch gene." Despite the questions, James continued to work hard and push through the fear, the doubt and the pain. As a result, in 2012, while playing for the Miami Heat, LeBron James, with the help of Dwyane Wade and Chris Bosh, finally won a NBA Championship. During post-game interviews, James and his teammates frequently noted that the defeat they experienced during the previous season's NBA Finals was the reason they were able to take home the Championship in 2012. In other words, their victory and success was born of the same strife that could have derailed their goals and dreams.

James' story provides a valuable lesson we can use as we navigate life and strive to be successful in following our dreams. The obstacles presented by defeat, at times, appear to be insurmountable. The rocks in the road appear to be bigger than nuggets and may even look like mountains; but in order to move mountains, we must first be able to handle the small stones in our lives.

While the trials and tribulations that we encounter may appear to be as big as boulders, they are just pebbles compared to the adversity that awaits us in the future. So you must conquer these stones knowing that it will prepare you to overcome the mountains that will undoubtedly arise throughout your life. In the pursuit of everything in life, we must experience and triumph over adversity in order to realize greatness. It was this triumph over adversity that led to one of the greatest moments in sports history.

On June 11, 1997, the Chicago Bulls played the Utah Jazz in Game 5 of the 1997 NBA Finals. In that game, Michael Jordan gave what is widely regarded as one of the greatest and most memorable athletic performances in the history of modern pro sports. Prior to and during the game, Jordan was suffering from the flu and experiencing nausea, aches, pains, and a 103-degree fever.

The best of seven series was tied at two games apiece and, despite his condition, Jordan refused to sit on the sideline, in the locker room or at home while his team took the court. Jordan somehow mustered the strength to not only compete, but also to dominate. He finished that game with 38 points, 7 rebounds, 5 assists, 3 steals, and 1 blocked shot, while leading the Bulls to victory and a 3-2 series lead.[9] The Bulls would go on to win the series and claim their fifth NBA Finals Championship in as many appearances.

Michael Jordan's accomplishment is a true example of greatness; greatness he was only able to achieve by overcoming a great obstacle and pushing past the pain. I'm in no way suggesting that you go play an NBA Finals game, a school-yard 3-on-3, or even go to work with the flu. As a matter of fact, go to the doctor, the pharmacist and then directly home. However, the point I'm trying to make is that although the circumstances that were before him were daunting, he overcame the obstacles and had an extremely successful performance. In moments like those where the task seems to be the greatest and we may even be at our weakest, we must continue to fight because these are the moments where we can reach our greatest levels of success.

Yes, it will be hard; yes it will hurt; and yes you may feel like giving up, but you can't. Even to this day, I too have hard days, but when I feel like it's too much, I think about the words I often heard from one of my coaches. My high school football coach, Coach Walt Frazier, used to always say that "pain is weakness leaving the body." I would always remark, under my breath of course, that it may also be a sign that something's wrong. Yet, over time, I realized what he was trying to say. Coach Frazier told us that in order to build muscle, the body needed to tear down fat and old muscle so it could build new muscle on top of it. He told us that is what happened every time we worked out, which explains the pain and the subsequent soreness.

The same can be said about us in our daily lives. In order for us to be stronger writers, speakers, readers, doctors, lawyers, athletes, musicians, engineers, teachers, pharmacists and people, we have to push past what we believe is our breaking point. We have to push past that moment where we stopped working the day before. We have to build upon the foundation of yesterday's workout, study session, research, or practice to go where we've never been, but have always wanted to go; further. To reach the pinnacle, we must push through the pain.

I was born into poverty, raised in the sewers
Streets always would be a part of me, it made me the truest.
And even when my days were the bluest
I never ran from adversity, instead ran to it.
Fear ain't in the heart of me I learned just do it.
You get courage in your fears right after you go through it."
-T.I. "Good Life"

CHAPTER 5 REFLECTIONS: STEP 4- PUSH THROUGH THE PAIN

1. DISCUSS A TIME IN YOUR LIFE WHEN YOU'VE BEEN CONFRONTED WITH A PAINFUL SITUATION.

2. WHAT DID YOU DO TO OVERCOME THAT SITUATION AND REACH YOUR GOAL?

3. WHAT OBSTACLES DO YOU ENVISION STANDING IN THE WAY OF YOU BEING SUCCESSFUL?

4. WHAT STANDS IN THE WAY OF MAKING YOUR DREAM COME TRUE?

5. WHAT WILL HELP YOU AND MOTIVATE YOU TO PUSH THROUGH THE PAIN?

CHAPTER 6: STEP 5- GIVE BACK

"Successful people are always looking for opportunities to help others. Unsuccessful people are always asking 'What's in it for me?'" -Brian Tracy

I like reading. Well I used to like reading until I went to law school. Being forced to read hundreds of pages of stuff you can't understand, and not knowing why you need to understand it, will do that to you. So, I'm definitely damaged now and may never be the same. Nonetheless, slowly but surely, I've redeveloped my passion for reading. When I do read, I like to read different things.

One of the things I like to read is the Bible. Whether you're Christian or not, there are a lot of good things that you can take from the Bible. One is the statement, which says, "To whom much is given, much is required." It means that those of us who have been blessed with much should give more than those who have been blessed with little. This principal isn't unique to Christianity. The notion that people who have much should share with those who do not is a tenet of many different faiths, parables and morality tales, therefore it shouldn't be dismissed as "just another passage from the Bible." While I read the Bible, you don't have to, but you should definitely take time to read because there are lessons to be learned in every book, magazine and periodical, if we just open our eyes and find them.

For example, many lessons can be learned from reading about Bill Gates. Gates is widely known for being one of the richest people in the world. However, before he earned the title, he too struggled. Despite scoring 1590 out of a possible 1600 on the SAT, Bill Gates never finished college. He dropped out of Harvard to start a company called Traf-O-Data, which eventually failed. It's easy to imagine that being a college dropout and a failed business owner may cause a person to be slightly, if not deeply, depressed. However, Gates did not let this setback stop him from pursuing his passion and striving to reach his goals in the computer industry.

In 1975, Bill Gates and Paul Allen founded Microsoft, which is the world's largest supplier and manufacturer of computer software today. The company has made Gates a billionaire many times over, but with that money came expectations. After being named the richest man in the world,

Gates stated that he wished he hadn't been given this title because of the attention and expectations that went along with it. However, over time, Gates began to appreciate the expectations others had of him when public opinion mounted suggesting that he could give more of his wealth to charity.

Gates studied the work of Andrew Carnegie and John D. Rockefeller to figure out the best way to give back. Andrew Carnegie, whom I mentioned earlier, was not only one of the world's greatest businessmen, but also one of the most important philanthropists of his era. He immigrated to the United States in 1848 with his parents and secured his first job as a factory worker. His last job, however, was owner of the Carnegie Steel Company, which he founded in the 1870s. By the 1890s, the company was the largest and most profitable industrial enterprise in the world. In 1901, Carnegie sold it to J.P. Morgan for $480 million, and Morgan subsequently created the company, U.S. Steel.

At the age of 66, Carnegie left a job that made him a billionaire by today's standards, adjusting for inflation, to engage in philanthropy full time. While his story epitomizes the term "rags to riches," it also is a great reminder of how we should live our lives. Carnegie believed that people should spend the first third of their lives getting all the education they can, the next third making all the money they can, and the last third giving it all away to worthy causes.[10] Carnegie's unique outlook on philanthropy and his charitable contributions ultimately inspired Bill Gates to give back.

In addition to Carnegie, John D. Rockefeller also inspired Bill Gates' philanthropic efforts. Rockefeller made his money in the oil business; as founder of the Standard Oil Company, and as the importance of gasoline grew, so did his wealth. He became the world's richest man and the first American worth more than a billion dollars. Adjusting for inflation, he is often regarded as the richest person in history. Rockefeller spent the last forty years of his life in retirement and used his fortune primarily to create the modern systematic approach of targeted philanthropy. He was able to do this through the creation of foundations that had a major impact on medicine, education, and scientific research.

Rockefeller founded both the University of Chicago and Rockefeller University. In 1884, he provided substantial funding for a college in Atlanta for Black women, which became Spelman College (named for Rockefeller's in-laws who were ardent abolitionists before the Civil War). In all that he did, Rockefeller followed John Wesley's dictum, "gain all you can, save all you can, and give all you can."[11] I believe we all should endeavor to follow in the philanthropic footsteps of Rockefeller and Carnegie and live out these principles in our daily lives, as Bill and Melinda Gates strive to do today.

Inspired and influenced by the lives of Carnegie and Rockefeller, in 1994, Bill Gates sold some of his Microsoft stock to create the William H. Gates Foundation. In 2000, Gates and his wife combined three family foundations into one and created the charitable Bill & Melinda Gates Foundation, which is the largest transparently-operated charitable foundation in the world. Unlike other major charitable organizations, the foundation allows benefactors to access information regarding how its money is being spent because its goal is to be open and honest about how its money is being allocated.

The generosity and extensive philanthropic efforts of David Rockefeller[12] have also been credited as a major influence in Gates' charitable giving. Gates and his father met with Rockefeller several times, and modeled their giving, in part, on the Rockefeller family's[13] philanthropic focus, namely those global problems that are ignored by governments and other organizations.

The primary aims of the Gates Foundation are, globally, to enhance healthcare and reduce extreme poverty, and in America, to expand educational opportunities and access to information technology. As of September 30, 2013 the Gates Foundation had an endowment of over $40 billion and, since its inception, it has supplied over $28 billion in grant payments.[14] Bill and Melinda Gates are some of the most generous philanthropists in America, having given over $28 billion to charitable causes. Eventually, they plan to give 95% of their wealth to charity.

Bill Gates' story is a great example of how important it is to give back. As a result of his generosity, billions of dollars will be given to scientific research to help advancements in healthcare and education all over the world. Gates' story is also an example of how contagious giving can be.

Gates' friend Warren Buffett is widely considered the most successful investor of the 20th century. He is the primary shareholder, chairman and CEO of Berkshire Hathaway, an American multinational conglomerate holding company that oversees and manages a number of subsidiary companies. The company wholly owns GEICO, BNSF, Lubrizol, Dairy Queen, Fruit of the Loom, Helzberg Diamonds, FlightSafety International, and NetJets, owns half of Heinz and an undisclosed percentage of Mars, Incorporated, and has significant minority holdings in American Express, The Coca-Cola Company, Wells Fargo, and IBM.[15] Buffett is consistently ranked among the world's wealthiest people: he was ranked as the world's wealthiest person in 2008 and was the third wealthiest person in the world as of 2011. In 2012, *Time* magazine named Buffett one of the most influential people in the world.

Aside from his wealth, Buffett is also well-known for his frugality or, in other words, for being cheap. He lives in the same house in Omaha, Nebraska that he purchased for $31,500 in 1958, which today is valued at approximately $700,000. In December 2006, it was reported that Buffett did not carry a cell phone, did not have a computer at his desk, and drove his own automobile, which is significantly different from most CEO's and billionaires today. While Buffett is frugal and keeps most of his money, he eventually decided to make a marked departure from his long-held beliefs of not giving to charity. In June 2006, he pledged to give the Bill & Melinda Gates Foundation approximately 10 million shares of his company, which was worth approximately $1.5 billion. Additionally, Buffett has also pledged to give away 99% of his wealth upon his death.[16] The fire started with Bill Gates and it spread to Warren Buffett. Who will catch it next?

Charity is contagious, but in a good way. This type of contagious syndrome means you don't have to worry about being vaccinated, quarantined, or wearing a surgical mask for the rest of your life. It takes courage to see a problem and then stand up and tackle that problem; courage which, unfortunately, not a lot of people possess. However, many of us will pitch in when we see others doing so. For example, many of us will walk past trash on the ground and not even think about picking it up. Yet, when we see others picking up trash, we will often lend a helping hand. It's like that insurance commercial that shows how one person doing the right thing, or doing something for someone else that they're not obligated to do, which inspires others. However, successful people don't wait to see if someone else will do the job. Successful people see that a job or service needs to be done and they do it. Don't wait and see if someone else will do what you know you should and could be doing because it may never happen. Get up and make it happen yourself; don't wait, just do it.

The Gates Foundation and others like it are necessary because an estimated 2 billion people worldwide are both poor and hungry.[17] In terms of poverty in the United States, a significant number of people are unable to eat, survive or live because the current minimum wage is $7.25 per hour.[18] In 2014, the official U.S. poverty level for a family of four was $23,850.[19] With a forty hour work week, a family of four with one minimum wage earner would earn $14,580, 61% of the poverty level.[20] In 2010, 46.9 million people lived in poverty, a rate of 15.1%, which is an increase from the 2007 level.[21] More than 20 million Americans live in extreme poverty, meaning that their family's income is less than half of the poverty line, which for a family of four is about $10,000.[22]

We live in a country with a lot of "haves", so much so that it's often easy to overlook the "have nots." While there are programs and policies in place to help ease the burden of hunger and poverty in America, such as the Supplemental Nutrition Assistance Program (SNAP)/Food stamps, the Special Supplemental Nutrition Program for Women, Infants and Children (WIC), the National School Lunch Program, the Earned Income Tax Credit (EITC) and Temporary Assistance to Needy Families (TANF), they're stop-gaps, not permanent solutions. Moreover, organizations such as The Salvation Army, Feeding America, Habitat for Humanity, and Ronald McDonald House Charities are designed to help meet the needs of those who are unable to meet their own. However, given what we know about increasing poverty, hunger, and homelessness, it is clear that these organizations are not enough; people like us need to do more and give more.

While most of us aren't billionaires or millionaires, we are able to give, and these organizations can use whatever donations we can spare. However, money isn't the only way you can give back. You can give back through your time and talent. You can give of your time by volunteering at places like Camillus House[23], which provides humanitarian services to the homeless and indigent population of Miami-Dade County, Florida or by supporting our troops through the Wounded Warriors Project[24], which provides programs and services to severely injured service members during the time between active duty and transition to civilian life. You can also give of your talent by helping kids learn to read at a local Boys & Girls Club, teaching them music or dance at a local YMCA/YWCA, or joining a mentoring program like Big Brothers/ Big Sisters. Remember, every little bit helps and that it's better to give a little than to not give anything at all.

I grew up in Miami- Dade County, a place more famous for its year-round warm weather, celebrities, and beautiful beaches than its crime, poverty and drug trafficking. Before the area of Northwest Miami-Dade County became the city of Miami Gardens in 2002, it was known as Carol City.

Carol City is home to the likes of Rick Ross, Flo Rida, NFL stars Santana and Sinorice Moss and the high school that boasts more NFL talent than any other high school in the country, Miami Carol City Senior High. While the area has a penchant for producing talent, it also has a penchant for producing teenage homicide victims. In 2007, the 33056 zip code was labeled the most dangerous zip code in Miami-Dade County. The twenty-two square mile area had a higher rate of gunshot deaths among children seventeen and younger than in any other part of the county.

Yet, for all of its negativity, it's still the city that I was born and raised in and if I had a say in the matter, I wouldn't want to have been born and raised anywhere else. I'm so very thankful for my experiences in this community. For a community that didn't have much to offer, it gave me everything that it had and because of my experiences, I give back every chance I get. My reward is the smile on people's faces when I'm helping to feed the homeless, sharing my time with needy kids, or motivating young people to follow their dreams. I consider it an honor and a privilege to give back because it's a testament to the fact that you are the author of your own story and that no matter how bad the setting is in the beginning, you can write a happy ending. I give back because my story is an example of how to overcome adverse circumstances and low expectations to ultimately become successful. I give back because charity is a sign of prosperity, a sign of achievement and, most importantly, it signifies that if I can do it so can you.

As people, we naturally subscribe to the theory of "me, myself and I" and "I'll get mine and you get yours the best way you can." We can't help it, we're born to be selfish. After all, self-preservation is the number one priority. However, just because we're born selfish doesn't mean that we can't live life self-lessly. Being overly concerned about self doesn't leave room for others to love or care about you. It's like a morbidly obese person standing in front of a small mirror, there isn't much room for anyone or anything else to be seen. The things that you do for others that bring laughter, smiles, and pure joy are the things that last, the things that matter. There's absolutely nothing wrong with loving yourself; in fact, I encourage you to do so. Unfortunately, the problem comes when you are in love with yourself because it doesn't allow you to love others, care for others or allow them to do the same for you.

As I mentioned earlier, my mother cared for my grandmother during her last few months on earth. It was an experience that lasted much longer than any of us, including the doctors, expected. It took a lot out of my mother to see her mother incapacitated, unable to care for herself, and dependent on her and medical professionals for even basic needs such as bathing. However, everything happens for a reason. One of the many things my mother said she took away from that experience is that you should be careful how you treat people because you never know how you're going to end up going out. To me, this means that you should be kind to those who you meet because before it's all said and done, you never know whose generosity and charity you may need.

Giving back is such an essential step in following your dreams because it's a sign of success. Albert Pike said, "What we have done for ourselves alone dies with us; what we have done for others and the world remains and is immortal." In essence, this means that truly successful people leave a legacy. For example, Wayne Gretzky will forever be remembered as one of the world's greatest hockey players. Rev. Dr. Martin Luther King, Jr., Mother Theresa and Mahatma Gandhi will be immortalized as three of the greatest humanitarians to ever live.

These successful people won't be remembered for the number of shoes in their closet, the expensive vacations they took, or the houses they owned. Instead, they'll be remembered for everything they did for their sport, in their profession and for the betterment of humanity, all the things they did that helped others.

The saying "it's better to give than to receive" is a tough concept to wrap your mind around, especially if you're like me and (really) enjoy receiving things. Who doesn't enjoy being treated to dinner at a fancy restaurant? Who doesn't like waking up on Christmas morning to a tree full of gifts? Who doesn't like going to work and being greeted with flowers by the delivery guy? If you said "not me" to any of these questions, either you're the most self-less person in the world or you need to have your head examined. Most people like to receive, yet giving back truly does feel good. Trust me, I've tried it and I like it. I really like it. But let's be clear, I also enjoy the feeling of going to the mall and being able to buy whatever I want. Although I like to buy things for myself, to be able to do something for someone else, a friend, a family member, or a stranger and see or hear their sheer joy is an amazing feeling. If you don't believe me, try it for yourself. See how it feels and tell me if it isn't one of the greatest feelings in the world.

Since we know that many people will always be poor, homeless, and hungry and that there will always be those among us who are less fortunate than others, when we become successful we have an obligation to help these individuals. These people don't have the means to single-handedly close the gaps between what they make and what they need, so we must provide the help they need; this is where we must step in and step up. Whether you have a little or a lot, if you have everything that you need and some leftover, you have more than a lot and enough to share. So, bottom line, be sure to give back.

"What we have done for ourselves alone dies with us; what we have done for others and the world remains and is immortal."
-Albert Pike

CHAPTER 6 REFLECTIONS: STEP 5- GIVE BACK

1. NAME 5 TALENTS, GIFTS AND ABILITIES THAT YOU HAVE

2. HOW CAN YOU USE THESE TO HELP OTHERS?

3. WHAT IS YOUR PLAN TO GIVE BACK?

4. WHY IS GIVING BACK IMPORTANT TO YOU?

CHAPTER 7: PUTTING IT ALL TOGETHER

Dream as if you'll live forever. Live as if you'll die today.
-James Dean

We live in a tough world and, perhaps, the people who have it the toughest are youth and young adults. Poverty, homelessness and hunger are all on the rise amongst youth. These days young adults face the tough decision of not whether they can go to college, trade/technical school or follow their dreams, but rather if they can afford to. The struggling economy, bleak job prospects and turmoil all over the world have led to some tough times and forced us to make some tough decisions in light of our circumstances.

It's easy to give up. It's easy to sit on the sidelines, shake our heads and believe all hope is lost. However, instead of looking at this as the time to give up and retreat, we should look at this as an opportunity to stand tall, hit the winning shot and show what we're truly made of. You can't win if you never get off the bench and into the game. Michael Jordan once said, "I can accept failure. Everyone fails at something. What I can't accept is not trying." Young people, despite the cloudy skies, now is not the time to stop trying. In fact, now is the time to work even harder and dig even deeper within yourself to reach your goals and follow your dreams.

We can't allow our circumstances to dictate our outcome because if we do, we will never win. Life is full of dire situations: death, taxes, your favorite team being ousted in the first round of the playoffs, layoffs, terrible grades, sickness, bad break-ups, etc. There will always be roadblocks, stop signs, walls, roadside ditches, and potholes and if you stopped, stalled, or quit every time you got to one, you would never reach your destination. Instead, you should choose to find a way through, over, or around them to continue on your road to success. Sir Winston Churchill stated, "Success is not final, failure is not fatal: it is the courage to continue that counts."

Remember that your road to success starts with believing in yourself. If you don't believe in you, there are no promises, assurances or even reasons for anyone else to believe in you. We must overcome our fear of failure and when it comes time to make a choice between standing and fighting for our dreams or turning and running, choose to stand and fight. Believe in yourself, your talent and your ability and you are well on your way down the road to success.

The next thing you need to do is make a plan. Just as you wouldn't walk up to Mike Tyson, Kimbo Slice, or the school bully and punch them in the face without a plan of attack, don't set out to accomplish anything without making a plan. Once you're armed with an unwavering confidence, make a plan to be successful. Without a blueprint, a house may never get built and if it does, it's surely not a house I'd ever want to live in. Without a roadmap you may never reach your destination.

After you've established a strong belief in yourself, your talent and your ability and have made a plan, you then have to "Just do it!" Seems simple in theory but actually getting off the couch, into the gym and putting down the cookies, chips, salsa, soda, fruit punch and candy is so much harder. The only person that can make your dreams come true is you. You and you alone possess the ability to turn your ideas into reality. If you don't do it, it can't happen.

While doing all of this, know that you will definitely, absolutely encounter obstacles and that you will definitely experience setbacks. At some point or another it will definitely hurt; and before it's all said and done, you'll definitely contemplate giving up at least one hundred times or more. When you contemplate giving up one hundred times, you have to overcome that urge one hundred times. What you have to do is develop the courage, the strength and the fortitude to push through the pain.

Once you've done all of that and you've reached your pinnacle of success, give back. Give back to those who helped you get to where you are, whether it's a school, a community, a local YMCA, your family and friends or all of the above. Giving back is a sign of prosperity and humility. Remember, giving back is about more than just writing a check. Giving back means giving your money, time, talent and ability to those who need it most.

I hope that you've found this book to be helpful, enjoyable and at the very least bearable. I hope that you will take the helpful tips, advice and examples of success and use them as guidelines by which to pattern your own success. At the end of the day, you are the author of your own story. Despite my supreme fascination with successful people and their stories, I can't make them my own. I can only use them as reference points as I write my own story.

Remember the four common traits of successful people: 1. They've all encountered adversity and overcome it to achieve success; 2. They have an uncanny ability to deal with whatever comes their way and maintain focus on their goals; 3. They have a firm belief in themselves, their talent and their ability; 4. They desire to control and therefore exercise that control over the things that can be controlled in their environment. Keep these traits in mind, use the five steps to follow your dreams and you'll be well on your way to turning your dreams into reality. My hope, my prayer, my desire for you is that you'll take my advice and follow your dreams. Stay up and be blessed!

"Every great dream begins with a dreamer. Always remember, you have within you the strength, the patience, and the passion to reach for the stars to change the world."
-Harriet Tubman

CHAPTER 7 REFLECTIONS: PUTTING IT ALL TOGETHER

1. WHAT ARE THE FOUR COMMON TRAITS OF SUCCESSFUL PEOPLE?

2. WHAT ARE THE FIVE STEPS TO FOLLOWING YOUR DREAMS?

3. HOW DO THE TWO WORK TOGETHER?

4. WHAT MUST YOU DO TO "PUT IT ALL TOGETHER?"

5. NOW THAT YOU'VE READ THIS BOOK, HOW WILL YOU APPLY IT TO YOUR LIFE?

6. WHAT'S NEXT?

[1] Dream. (n.d.). In *Dictionary.reference.com*. Retrieved from http://dictionary.reference.com/browse/dream

[2] Dream. (n.d.). Retrieved July 6, 2012 from the Dream Wiki: http://en.wikipedia.org/wiki/Dream

[3] Andrew Carnegie. (n.d.). Retrieved July 11, 2012 from the Andrew Carnegie Wiki: http://en.wikipedia.org/wiki/Andrew_Carnegie

[4] Hill, Napoleon (2008). The Law of Success.

[5] Fear. (n.d.). In *Dictionary.reference.com*. Retrieved from http://dictionary.reference.com/browse/fear?s=t

[6] Fear. (n.d.). Retrieved July 7, 2012 from the Fear Wiki: http://en.wikipedia.org/wiki/Fear

[7] Nike. (2012) http://nikeinc.com/

[8] Nike, Inc. Retrieved from the Nike, Inc. Wiki: http://en.wikipedia.org/wiki/Nike,_Inc.

[9] Weinberg, Rick (2004). "79: Jordan battles flu, makes Jazz sick". ESPN. http://sports.espn.go.com/espn/espn25/story?page=moments/79.

[10] Andrew Carnegie. (n.d.). Retrieved July 11, 2012 from the Andrew Carnegie Wiki: http://en.wikipedia.org/wiki/Andrew_Carnegie

[11] John D. Rockefeller. (n.d.). Retrieved from the John D. Rockefeller Wiki: http://en.wikipedia.org/wiki/John_D._Rockefeller

[12] David Rockefeller, Sr. Current patriarch of the Rockefeller family and only surviving child of John D. Rockefeller, Jr. and only surviving grandchild of John D. Rockefeller, Sr. Retrieved from David Rockefeller Wiki: http://en.wikipedia.org/wiki/David_Rockefeller

[13] Rockefeller Foundation. http://www.rockefellerfoundation.org/

[14] Bill & Melinda Gates Foundation. Retrieved from the Gates Foundation Wiki: http://en.wikipedia.org/wiki/Gates_Foundation

[15] Berkshire Hathaway. http://www.berkshirehathaway.com/

[16] Bill & Melinda Gates Foundation. Retrieved from the Gates Foundation Wiki: http://en.wikipedia.org/wiki/Gates_Foundation

[17] World Hunger Facts. http://www.worldhunger.org/articles/Learn/world%20hunger%20facts%202002.htm

[18] United States Bureau of the Census. 2011a. "Poverty Thresholds." http://www.census.gov/hhes/www/poverty/data/threshld/index.html

[19] United States Department of Health and Human Services, Office of the Assistant Secretary for Planning and Evaluation. 2014. "2014 Poverty Guidelines" http://aspe.hhs.gov/poverty/14poverty.cfm

[20] United States Bureau of the Census. 2011a. "Poverty Thresholds." http://www.census.gov/hhes/www/poverty/data/threshld/index.html

[21] DeNavas-Walt, Carmen, Bernadette D. Proctor, and Jessica C. Smith. (2011) (p.14). U.S. Census Bureau, Current Population Reports, P60-

239. "Income, Poverty, and Health Insurance Coverage in the United States: 2010." U.S. Government Printing Office, Washington, DC, 2011 http://www.census.gov/prod/2011pubs/p60-239.pdf
[22] DeNavas-Walt, Carmen, Bernadette D. Proctor, and Jessica C. Smith. (2011) (p. 19). U.S. Census Bureau, Current Population Reports, P60-239. "Income, Poverty, and Health Insurance Coverage in the United States: 2010." U.S. Government Printing Office, Washington, DC, 2011 http://www.census.gov/prod/2011pubs/p60-239.pdf
[23] Camillus House (2012) http://www.camillus.org/
[24] Wounded Warriors Project, (2011) http://www.woundedwarriorproject.org/